Do You KNOW?™

THE CHICAGO BEARS

A hard-hitting quiz for tailgaters, ~~fo~~ haters, armchair quarterbacks, and anyone who'd kill for their team

Guy Robinson

SOURCEBOOKS, INC.®
NAPERVILLE, ILLINOIS

Published by Sourcebooks, Inc.
P.O. Box 4410, Naperville, Illinois 60567-4410
(630) 961-3900
Fax: (630) 961-2168
www.sourcebooks.com

Printed and bound in the United States of America
SP 10 9 8 7 6 5 4 3 2

This is the kind of quiz that will make you dig deep into the football compartment of your brain. If you *really* know the Bears and their history, you'll be able to answer questions about classic games you were lucky enough to see while they happened, historic series you've watched on DVD, and unbelievable plays you've heard about so often you've come to think you were on the field yourself. You'll know about winning coaches and losing coaches, celebrated passers and legendary runners, thrilling playoff games and enduring records, special rivalries and favorite traditions—the stuff of countless game days and time afterward sitting around arguing about whether he ever should've gone for the Hail Mary and whose defense was *really* impenetrable.

You should find that some of the answers pop readily to mind. Others will be a true challenge. And however good you think you are, you can expect to face a few that will stop you cold. That's part of the fun.

So here are 100 questions. Count ten points for each correct answer. Where a question has more than one part, you'll be told how to divide the credit. Here and there you'll find a chance to earn five or ten bonus points, so it's theoretically possible to score more than 1,000. (But you won't!)

Figure your performance this way:

Above 900:	**Spectacular!**
700–899:	A very solid showing.
500–699:	Nothing to be ashamed of.
Below 500:	Told you it was tough.

1. **During the 1980s, how did quarterback Jim McMahon celebrate a score?**

    a. He high-fived every player on the field.
    b. He head-butted the offensive linemen.
    c. He performed a version of the "Lambeau Leap" called the "Soldier Slide."
    d. He dropped to one knee and bowed toward the opposition stands.

2. **Before George Halas hired ex-Bears tight end Mike Ditka as head coach, he checked with Ditka's boss. Who was that?**

    T_____ L_____

3. **Which of these *wasn't* a nickname for Red Grange?**

    a. "The Galloping Ghost"
    b. "The Wheaton Iceman"
    c. "77"
    d. "The Lone Granger"

4. **And what was Grange's real first name?** _____

5. **Speaking of first names, for five points each what were the first names of these guys?**

    a. Buddy Ryan: _____
    b. Paddy Driscoll: _____

6. **Not that anyone is supposed to know every player's *middle* name, but what goes between "Richard" and "Butkus"? Perhaps the initial will help.**

    Richard M_____ Butkus

7. Who was the first Bears coach to end his term with a losing record?

J_____ D_____

8. Which Bear was the first football player whose image appeared on the front of a Wheaties box?

   a. Bill George
   b. George Halas
   c. Sid Luckman
   d. Walter Payton
   e. Brian Urlacher

9. What did the Decatur Staleys have to do with Chicago Bears history?

_____

10. They called me "The Kansas Comet." I may have been Chicago's best runner ever, right out of the gate—I was the unanimous choice for NFL Rookie of the Year. Eventually my knees gave out and I left the game after the 1971 season. I made it to the Pro Football Hall of Fame at age 34. Who am I?

_____

11. Other Bears, other nicknames. For two points each, match them:

   a. "Samurai"   f. Ed Sprinkle
   b. "The Claw"   g. Kevin Butler
   c. "Butthead"   h. Clyde Turner
   d. "The Brute"   i. Mike Singletary
   e. "Bulldog"   j. George Trafton

12. Finish the lyric:

   We're not here to start no trouble…

   _____

13. What Bear linebacker was mentioned in gossip columns and blogs after he was seen hanging with Paris Hilton in Las Vegas and she was seen at a Bears game wearing his jersey? (Hint: Some call him the most overrated player in the NFL.)

   _____

14. That jersey Paris was wearing—what number was it? _____

15. In 1986, a certain Green Bay Packer took out Jim McMahon with a late hit that messed up his shoulder, ending the Punky QB's season and, some believe, the Bears' chances for that year's Super Bowl. Who was that certain Packer? (For five bonus points, how did the perp indicate that he was on the prowl for Bear blood? For five more, what penalty was ultimately passed down?)

   C_____ M_____

16. For five points each, who made popular the "46 Defense" and where'd that name come from?

   _____
   _____

17. Which Bears defensive standout was sometimes called "The Heart of the Defense"?

   _____

18. **For two points each, figure out which Bear player or coach said each quote.**

   a. "I wouldn't ever set out to hurt anybody deliberately unless it was, you know, important—like a league game or something."

   b. "If I'm not selected for the Pro Bowl this year, Stevie Wonder must be counting the ballots."

   c. "Some teams are named Smith, some Grabowski. We're Grabowskis."

   d. "Even when I was little I was big."

   e. "San Francisco has always been my favorite booing city.... One time in Kezar Stadium they gave me a standing boo."

   f. William "The Refrigerator" Perry

   g. George Halas

   h. Otis Wilson

   i. Mike Ditka

   j. Dick Butkus

19. **For five points apiece, what members of the mid-'80s Junkyard Dog Defense introduced woofing to the Bears and their fans?**

   D_____   D_____
   O_____   W_____

20. **Here's a bit of regular dialog between the public address man and fans at Soldier Field. You fill in the fans' lines.**

   "There's a timeout..."
   "_____?"
   "...On the field."
   "_____!"

21. **In one memorable championship game, a referee asked the Bears not to try any more kicks for extra points. Why? (Hint: Their opponents? The Washington Redskins. The year? 1940.)**

   _____

22. To what did many attribute that victory?

a. The Bears had begun using a new sports drink.
b. The Bears used a variation of the T-formation.
c. The Redskins had lost eight players to dysentery.
d. The Redskins coach had overslept and missed the game.

23. Earlier that same year, the Skins beat the Bears 7–3. What happened during that game that angered the Bears and their fans?

a. A fan streaked across the field just before a crucial fourth-down play.
b. A Washington tackle knocked Sid Luckman unconscious with a late hit.
c. Redskins fans sang "The Teddy Bears' Picnic" throughout the game.
d. The ref didn't call pass interference on the game's last play.

24. Which of these statements about Mike Ditka *isn't* true?

a. After he played with the Bears, he played with Philadelphia and Dallas.
b. For several years while he was coaching he studied cello.
c. He had a heart attack during the 1988 season but missed no games.
d. His restaurants offer a dish called "Da Pork Chop."
e. He once licensed a computer game called "Mike Ditka's Ultimate Football."

25. The Bears refer to fans not as "The 12th Man" but as:

"The _____"

26. For two points each, match the Bears and their college alma maters:

a. Gary Fencik   f. Michigan
b. Sid Luckman   g. Columbia
c. Jim Harbaugh   h. Arkansas
d. Walter Payton   i. Yale
e. Dan Hampton   j. Jackson State

27. The team's fight song dates to 1941. It's still played and sung after every Bears score. What's it called?

"_____, _____"

28. Where are the Bears' practice facilities?

   a. An unnamed private island in Lake Michigan
   b. Lake Forest, IL
   c. Lambeau Field
   d. Soldier Field

29. What actor-screenwriter named his bull mastiff after a Bears linebacker and featured the dog in a couple of his movies? (Five points for the name of the movie man, five for the dog.)

_____

_____

30. For two points each, match the players and their retired numbers:

   a. 3   f. Walter Payton
   b. 34   g. Dick Butkus
   c. 41   h. Bill Hewitt
   d. 51   i. Bronko Nagurski
   e. 56   j. Brian Piccolo

31. Security personnel at Soldier Field games wear:

   a. red carnations
   b. bear heads
   c. blue and orange jackets
   d. red jackets or shirts

32. Which Bears great appeared in a 12-episode movie serial with Francis X. Bushman and Stepin Fetchit? (The title would give it away.)

_____

33. Who were Bill Swerski, Todd O'Connor, Pat Arnold, and Carl Wollarski? (For five bonus points, what organization did they frequently toast?)

_____

34. The 1969 season was not a good one for the Bears, unless you consider 1–13 a fine performance. The one team they did manage to beat that year—a team that also finished with a 1–13 record—was the:

a. Atlanta Falcons   c. San Francisco 49ers
b. Pittsburgh Steelers   d. St. Louis Cardinals

35. What's the name of the Bears' mascot?

_____

36. What number jersey is worn by "Bearman," the fan known for attending games wearing a stuffed bear head and bear paws?

_____

37. George Blanda's lengthy career touched four different decades. The first phase was spent with the Bears, chiefly as a quarterback and kicker. He later played with the Houston Oilers and the Oakland Raiders. Within two years, how old was he when he finally, at last, retired?

_____

38. "The Refrigerator" may have weighed 300-some pounds, but he could still:

    a. run the 100-meter dash in 12 seconds
    b. dunk a basketball
    c. turn cartwheels
    d. marathon square dance

39. Dick Butkus ended his playing career in 1973 because of:

    a. knee injuries
    b. a back injury
    c. drug accusations
    d. a divorce and other personal stresses

40. What team did the Bears defeat in the "Fog Bowl," the 1988 NFL playoff game, when the stadium by the lake was so shrouded in dense fog that players couldn't see as far as the sidelines and fans and play-by-play announcers in the press box often didn't know what was going on? (Ten extra points for that day's score.)

_____

41. The bear head that appears on team flags and pennants:

    a. faces right
    b. faces left
    c. faces front with its mouth open
    d. faces front with its mouth closed

42. For a few seasons during his long reign, George Halas turned the head coach position over to assistants Hunk Anderson and Luke Johnsos. Why?

_____

43. In 1925, Red Grange made the cover of a two-year-old magazine named *Time*. More than 60 years later, *two* grinning Chicago players were on the magazine's front behind the headline "Super Bowl XX: Bad News Bears." For five points apiece, name those cover boys.

_____

_____

44. In 1985, NFL Commissioner Pete Rozelle fined Jim McMahon $5,000 for wearing a headband bearing a sponsor's name (Adidas) during a divisional playoff game. What did McMahon do to retaliate?

_____

45. Many years later, in 2007, Brian Urlacher made a similar transgression and was hit with a much heftier fine—$100,000— for wearing an unauthorized commercial cap to Media Day before Super Bowl XLI. What did his cap promote?

   a. Nike
   b. Slim-Fast
   c. Vitaminwater
   d. Domino's Pizza
   e. Special Olympics

46. George Halas said that trading this star University of Texas quarterback after his rookie season was "the worst deal I ever made." That could be—the ex-Bear went on to a brilliant career in Detroit and Pittsburgh. Who was he?

   B_____ L_____

47. "All the pieces are in place to make a run deep into the playoffs." Who said it and then had to try to live it down? (Hint: Think 1996.)

_____

48. He won a Golden Globe award and other kudos for playing an aging actor adrift in Tokyo who meets a photographer's wife in the same boat. He's done other dramatic film roles. Still, he's better known for making people laugh. In real life, he's known as a huge Bears fan. Who is he?

_____

49. In his second year as a Bear, he returned an interception for a winning touchdown in overtime. Then, in the very next game, he did it again. Who? (Ten bonus points for each opponent)

_____

50. The cheerleaders who entertained fans and led the rooting for the Bears for nearly a decade were known as the:
    a. Sweet Bears
    b. Honey Bears
    c. Bearesses
    d. brunettes

51. Why didn't the Bears' Super Bowl championship team follow tradition and visit the White House in January 1986?

_____

52. The Bears ended the 1969 season with a 1–13 record. So did the Pittsburgh Steelers. The Steelers won the toss that determined the first draft pick of 1970; they chose Terry Bradshaw. The Bears traded their pick to the:

   a. Buffalo Bills
   b. Cleveland Browns
   c. Green Bay Packers
   d. Philadelphia Eagles

53. In 1997, the Bears again gave up their first-round draft pick—this time to the Seattle Seahawks in exchange for a quarterback who lasted one season in Chicago. Name him. (Ten bonus points: During that season, how many touchdowns did he score for the Bears?)

   R_____ M_____

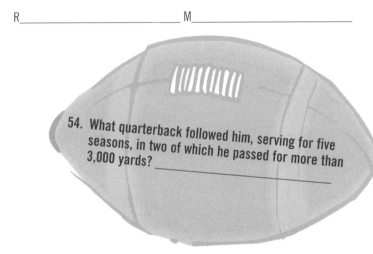

54. What quarterback followed him, serving for five seasons, in two of which he passed for more than 3,000 yards? _____

55. I replaced "Sweetness" and soon started to thrill fans with my agile rushing and my leaps into the end zone. I wore No. 35. For part of one year I held out for a salary increase. Who am I?

   _____

56. Where did the Bears play longer, the old Soldier Field or Wrigley Field?

_____

57. At the new Soldier Field, tailgaters gather at South Lot and at _____ Deck.

58. Alonzo Spellman had five pretty good years with the Bears in the '90s, but after some floundering he regrouped to focus on:

  a. his investments   c. golf
  b. portrait painting   d. mixed martial arts

59. At the time, it was the most lopsided Super Bowl score ever. That was January 1986, the double-X Big Game, the one in which the Bears humiliated the Pats. OK, now the score:

_____

60. Which of these statements about George "Papa Bear" Halas *isn't* true?

  a. He once played the outfield with the New York Yankees.
  b. He took the navy and orange of his college team for the Bears' uniforms.
  c. He has appeared on a United States postage stamp.
  d. Fifty years separate his first Bears championship and his last.
  e. He coached his last game at age 72.

61. Before he joined the Bears, Cedric Benson played baseball with the Rookie League team of which Major League baseball franchise?

  a. The Los Angeles Dodgers
  b. The Baltimore Orioles
  c. The St. Louis Cardinals
  d. The Florida Marlins

62. **Walter Payton's single-game rushing record, set against the Vikings in 1977, stood for nearly 23 years until it was broken by Corey Dillon. What was Payton's game total?**

_____

63. **Payton died at age 45 of:**

   a. heart disease
   b. liver disease
   c. burns suffered in a house fire
   d. unknown causes

64. **Bears games on radio were handled for many years by a newspaper gossip columnist and a sports announcer known as the TV voice of the Chicago Cubs. For five points each, name them.**

   I_____ K_____
   J_____ B_____

65. **During his time with the Bears, Tank Johnson was _not_ reported to have been charged with:**

   a. gambling
   b. violation of gun laws
   c. violation of probation
   d. resisting arrest

66. **For two points each, match the books and their authors:**

   a. _Flesh and Blood_   f. Mike Ditka
   b. _Never Die Easy_   g. Gale Sayers
   c. _In Life, First You Kick Ass_ h. Dick Butkus
   d. _I Am Third_   i. Mike Singletary
   e. _Calling the Shots_   j. Walter Payton

67. Who *didn't* make it into the Pro Football Hall of Fame with the first class of inductees, in 1963?

   a. Red Grange
   b. George Halas
   c. Sid Luckman
   d. Bronko Nagurski

68. OK, so he wasn't inducted in 1963. When *did* he get in?

   _____

69. He was a Bears tight end and wide receiver for eight seasons in the '80s. In the 21st century, his son spent several years as a wide receiver for the Indianapolis Colts. Name the father, a member of Chicago's first Super Bowl team.

   E_____ M_____

70. Soldier Field, 1991. The Bears trail the Jets 13–6, fourth down and less than a minute to go. Harbaugh aims for Anderson and boom! Extra point by Butler and…overtime! The Jets muff a field goal attempt and it's the Bears' turn again. This time, a Harbaugh pass to Cap Boso, who jumps up from the end zone with a face full of grass. The players head for the lockers. But wait. Instant replay and—no, the ruling is that Boso's knee hit dirt on the one before he went in. What happens next?

   _____

   _____

71. For five points each, who plays Brian Piccolo and Gale Sayers in *Brian's Song*, the much-remembered made-for-TV movie about the two best-friend Bears?

_____ as Piccolo

_____ as Sayers

72. How many Pro Bowl MVP awards did Sayers win? _____

73. Five points for Piccolo's college, five for the school where Sayers was a two-time All-American.

Piccolo: _____

Sayers: _____

74. In 1990, the Bears wore U.S. flag decals on their helmets as a nod to U.S. troops serving in the first Gulf War. The next year, during the last games of the season and playoffs their helmets carried a football-shaped patch with the number 91. Why?

_____

75. What's on the left uniform sleeve of all Bears players, and why?

_____

76. Lovie Smith is a noted supported of organizations that combat:

a. leukemia   c. diabetes
b. AIDS   d. alopecia

77. Before Smith began coaching, for what NFL team did he play?

_____

78. **Besides being one of the most-honored football players of the 20th century, Bronko Nagurski was:**

   a. a major league baseball player
   b. a professional wrestler
   c. a big band crooner
   d. a stand-up comic

79. **And what defensive tackle who was a Bear from 1981 to 1993 took up the same line of off-field work as Nagurski? (Ten bonus points: What was his nickname?)**

   _____

80. **Who *didn't* spend his entire NFL playing career in a Bears uniform?**

   a. Jerry Azumah
   b. Joe Fortunato
   c. Keith Van Horn
   d. Dave Whitsell

81. **Mike Ditka is known for his off-key version of what song, performed at a sporting event in what location?**

   " _____ " sung at

   _____

82. **I was a defensive tackle for the Vikings and the Bears for 15 seasons, never missed a regular season game, and was elected to the Pro Football Hall of Fame. While I was at it, I earned a law degree, which is how I ended up on the Minnesota Supreme Court. Who am I?**

   A_____ P_____

83. Five more quotes for you to match. Two points apiece.

a. "I don't care how complicated they make the game seem, it's really based on two principles, and those are blocking and tackling."

b. "Football kickers are like taxicabs. You can always go out and hire another one."

c. "Most football players are temperamental. That's 90 percent temper and 10 percent mental."

d. "I think there is less enjoyment now. The quarterback always handles the ball. The game always seems the same. Only the names and numbers change—and the platoons. Remember, we only played with 18 men."

e. "A lot of fans were drawn to me because they knew that whatever the score was, I was going to run as hard as I could on every play. You don't have that now; you have guys waiting for next week or even next year."

f. Doug Plank
g. Red Grange
h. Walter Payton
i. Bronko Nagurski
j. Buddy Ryan

84. Chicago was the first league team to go unbeaten and untied in a regular season, 13–0–0. In what year?

a. 1934
b. 1941
c. 1942
d. 1985
e. 2006

85. Undefeated in the regular season that year, yes, but they lost the championship. To whom?

_____

86. During that championship game, the icy ground made solid footing almost impossible for both sides. What did the opponents do in the second half that enabled them to beat the Bears 30–13 with a better-than-expected running game?

_____

87. What was the one-word name of the fan who used to lead cheers at Soldier Field dressed in a No. 1 Bears jersey and carrying a megaphone?

_____

88. Gabe Reid was the first NFL player from:

a. Guam
b. South Africa
c. Tasmania
d. American Samoa

89. At one time, by NFL rules, passes had to be thrown from at least five yards behind the line of scrimmage. A rule change allowing a pass from anywhere behind the line was enacted after a pass by a Bear fullback caused controversy in the 1932 championship game. The rule now is informally named after that back. What's it called?

_____

90. The Bears' old nickname, "Monsters of the Midway," was derived in the 1940s from a university after the school abolished its football program. What university?

_____

91. Who was Jim Finks and what did he do in 1982?

_____

_____

92. What Bear quarterback was first in the NFL to toss seven TD passes in one game?

    a. Rex Grossman   c. Sid Luckman
    b. Erik Kramer   d. Jim McMahon

93. Mike Singletary was a college All-America honoree both as a junior and as a senior while playing for a university team also known as the Bears (although not as Da Bearss). Which university?

    a. Baylor   c. Central Arkansas
    b. Brown   d. Missouri State

94. During a 1992 Vikings game at Minneapolis, Coach Ditka let fly at quarterback Jim Harbaugh in an outburst that was repeatedly recapped on the tube and is still remembered and discussed. What caused Ditka to lose it?

_____

_____

95. Where did Buddy Ryan go after he left the Bears?

    a. Houston Oilers   c. Oklahoma State
    b. Minnesota Vikings   d. Philadelphia Eagles

96. Why didn't Dave McGinnis take the job as head coach of the Bears in 1999?

_____

97. Pick the one quote *not* attributed to Ditka:

    a. "If you're not in the parade, you watch the parade. That's life."

    b. "Success isn't permanent and failure isn't fatal; it's the courage to continue that counts."

    c. "What's the difference between a three-week-old puppy and a sportswriter? In six weeks, the puppy stops whining."

    d. "Every time you win, you're reborn. When you lose, you die a little."

    e. "Effort without talent is a depressing situation, but talent without effort is a tragedy."

98. It's a classic football tale, told and retold for decades, from the days when players played *really* rough. It's about one of the greats. He takes the ball, heads toward the opposition goal, knocks one defender unconscious, breaks another's shoulder, hits the post, bounces off it, and stops only when he crashes into a brick wall at the back of the end zone...and cracks the wall. A coach runs over. "Watch that last guy," the runner mumbles. "He hits pretty hard." Who's the subject of this story?

_____

99. Since 1967, the Associated Press has named a Rookie of the Year in the offensive and defensive categories. In the 20th century, Bears rookies took just two of those awards, both for defense. Can the players' initials and their rookie years help you earn five points apiece?

W_____ C_____ (1973)

M_____ C_____ (1990)

100. Who's responsible for "The Curse of the Honey Bears"?

    a. Virginia McCaskey   c. Pete Rozelle

    b. George McCaskey   d. The Honey Bears

ANSWERS

1. b.

2. Tom Landry (head coach of the Dallas Cowboys, for whom Ditka worked as an assistant)

3. d.

4. Harold

5. a. James, b. John

6. Marvin

7. The man who followed George Halas in 1968, Jim Dooley

8. d.

9. That was the team's name for its first two years, derived from the sponsor, A.E. Staley, a corn processing company in Decatur, Illinois

10. Gale Sayers

11. a.-i., b.-f., c.-g., d.-j., e.-h.

12. *We're just here to do the Super Bowl Shuffle* (from the novelty rap number a band of Bears recorded en route to Super Bowl XX)

13. Brian Urlacher

14. 54

15. Charles Martin (bonus: during the game he wore a hand towel printed with a list of the jersey numbers of several Chicago players—presumably targets for the day—with McMahon's at the top; Martin was ejected from the game and suspended for two more)

16. Buddy Ryan, the Bears' defensive coordinator; from safety Doug Plank's uniform number

17. Mike Singletary

18. a.-j., b.-h., c.-i., d.-f., e.-g.

19. Dave Duerson and Otis Wilson

20. *"There's a timeout…"*
    "Where?"
    "…On the field."
    "Ohhhhh!"

21. In that contest, which Chicago won in a blowout (73–0), extra-point balls were being kept by fans in the end zone stands and the refs were down to their last football

22. b.

23. d.

24. b.

25. Fourth Phase

26. a.-i., b.-g., c.-f., d.-j., e.-h.

27. "Bear Down, Chicago Bears"
28. b.
29. Sylvester Stallone, Butkus (*Rocky* and *Rocky II*)
30. a.-i., b.-f., c.-j., d.-g., e.-h.
31. d.
32. Red Grange, who appeared in a serial with a title derived from his nickname, *The Galloping Ghost*
33. Characters on "Bill Swerski's Superfans," a recurring sketch on *Saturday Night Live* (bonus: "*Da* Bears!")
34. b.
35. Staley Da Bear
36. Doug Plank's No. 46
37. Blanda called it quits at 48
38. b.
39. a.
40. The Philadelphia Eagles (extra points: 20-12)
41. c.
42. Halas was serving in the military during World War II
43. "The Refrigerator" and "Sweetness," William Perry and Walter Payton
44. He showed up to the NFC title game wearing a headband emblazoned "ROZELLE"
45. c.
46. Bobby Layne
47. Head coach Dave Wannstedt, whose season ended 7-9
48. Bill Murray
49. Mike Brown did that in 2001 (bonus: San Francisco 49ers, 37-31, and Cleveland Browns, 27-21)
50. b.
51. Because two days after the game, the space shuttle *Challenger* blew up in midair, killing its crew
52. c.
53. Rick Mirer (bonus: zero)
54. Erik Kramer
55. Neal Anderson
56. Wrigley 1921-70, Soldier 1971-2001 (you do the math)

57. Waldron

58. d.

59. 46–10

60. d. (42 years)

61. a.

62. 275 yards

63. b.

64. Irv Kupcinet and Jack Brickhouse

65. a.

66. a.-h., b.-j., c.-f., d.-g., e.-i.

67. c.

68. 1965

69. Emery Moorehead

70. The teams regroup on the field for one more play; Harbaugh scores on a short sneak for a 19–13 victory

71. James Caan as Piccolo, Billy Dee Williams as Sayers

72. He played in four Pro Bowls and won three MVP awards: 1966, 1967, and 1969

73. Piccolo, Wake Forest; Sayers, University of Kansas

74. In memory of teammate Fred Washington, a rookie defensive tackle who was killed in a car crash just before Christmas

75. "GSH," the initials of founder-owner-manager George Stanley Halas

76. c.

77. For no team: after college play at the University of Tulsa, he went straight to coaching—high school, college, and then pro

78. b.

79. Steve McMichael (bonus: Mongo)

80. d. (Whitsell spent time with Detroit before and New Orleans after his six seasons as a Bear)

81. "Take Me Out to the Ballgame," during the seventh-inning stretch at Wrigley Field

82. Alan Page

83. a.-g., b.-j., c.-f., d.-i., e.-h.

84. a.

85. The New York Giants (8–5–0 for the season)

86. Several Giants players changed from cleats to sneakers borrowed from a nearby college, which is why the match is sometimes called "The Sneakers Game"

87. Rocky

88. d.

89. "The Bronko Nagurski Rule"

90. The University of Chicago

91. Bears general manager and executive vice president; he resigned because owner George Halas hired Mike Ditka as head coach without consulting him

92. c.

93. a.

94. With Chicago in the lead 20–0, Harbaugh ignored instructions and called an audible that intended receiver Neal Anderson didn't hear in a noisy Metrodome; the resulting interception turned into a TD that led to a run of 21 straight Vikings points and a final score of 21–20; Ditka was not happy

95. d. (as head coach)

96. Because management called a press conference to announce his hiring before he had accepted

97. d. (from George Allen)

98. Bronko Nagurski

99. Wally Chambers and Mark Carrier

100. a. Right after the win in Super Bowl XX, owner McCaskey disbanded the cheerleaders, leading some superstitious folks to forecast that the Bears would never win another until the Honey Bears are back on the sidelines